CITIES

MARKE

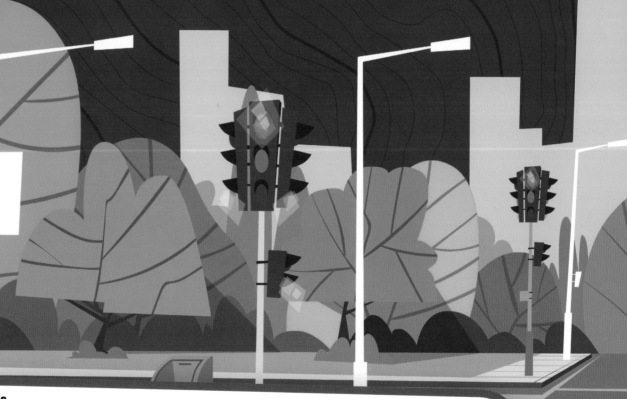

BookLife
PUBLISHING

©2019
BookLife Publishing Ltd.
King's Lynn
Norfolk, PE30 4LS

ISBN: 978-1-78637-863-7

Written by:
William Anthony

Edited by:
John Wood

Designed by:
Amy Li

CONTENTS

Words that look like <u>this</u> can be found in the glossary on page 24.

SUPER STATS

Numbers are everywhere. They help us <u>compare</u> lots of different things so we can find out all sorts of information, such as which is the largest, smallest, tallest or oldest.

10

5

FACT

Stats is short for the word statistics. Statistics are numbers that <u>represent</u> bits of information.

8

2

4

CITIES

Cities are some of the busiest and most impressive places that humans live in. They can be big or small, have lots of people or very few, be hot or cold, and even have more bicycles than humans.

LARGEST POPULATION

Cities are usually areas in a country where large numbers of people live. Some cities are home to millions of people. The total number of people that live in one area is called the population. Towns, cities, countries and continents all have populations.

FACT

In the past, a town in the UK could only become a city if it had a <u>cathedral.</u>

The biggest city in the world by its population is Tokyo, Japan. Over **37 million** people live there. These are the top five largest cities in the world by population:

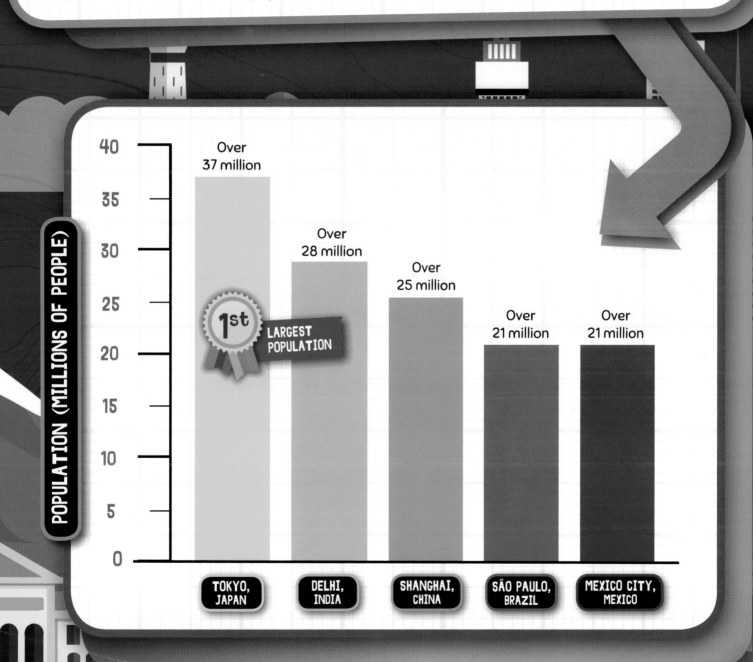

SMALL CAPITAL CITIES

A capital city is usually where a country's <u>government</u> can be found. The biggest decisions for a country are made in a capital city.

South Africa

STAT ATTACK!

Some countries have more than one capital. South Africa has the most capital cities, with 3 (Cape Town, Pretoria and Bloemfontein).

There are lots of capital cities with very small populations. The capital city of Palau is called Ngerulmud, and it is home to around **400** people. That's smaller than many schools! Here are some more small capital city populations from around the world:

SMALLEST CAPITAL CITY

1st

NGERULMUD, PALAU
Around **400** people

Palau flag

VATICAN CITY, STATE OF VATICAN CITY
Around **800** people

YAREN, NAURU
Around **1,100** people

FUNAFUTI, TUVALU
Around **4,500** people

SAN MARINO, SAN MARINO
Around **4,500** people

BIGGEST CITY

Another way of measuring the size of a city is by how much space it covers. We can use a measurement of <u>square kilometres</u> to do this. A city that covers a lot of space doesn't mean that it has a bigger population.

STAT ATTACK!

New York City covers the largest area of any city but only has a population of around **8.5 million**. That's much smaller than the cities on page 7.

TAXI

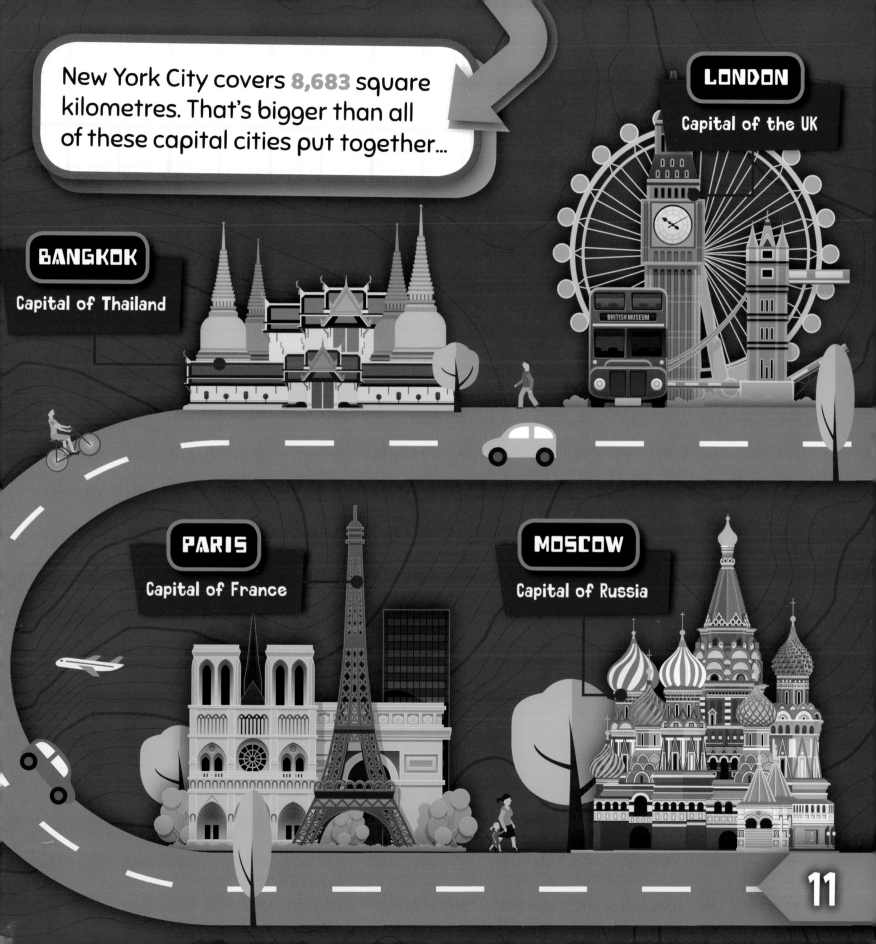

MOST THUNDERSTORMS IN THE US

Some cities must cope with worse weather than others. Some cities flood a lot, while others deal with lots of wind. Many cities in the US get lots of thunderstorms.

FACT

Most thunderstorms in the US happen in the southeast of the country.

LIVE

NEWS — THUNDERSTORMS IN THE SOUTHEAST

To measure how stormy a city is, we can count how many days in a year that a storm happens. The stormiest city in the US is Fort Myers, in Florida. Out of the 365 days in a year, Fort Myers usually has around 88 days of thunderstorms.

FACT

That's almost <u>one-quarter</u> of the year!

THUNDERSTORMS 88 DAYS

NO THUNDERSTORMS 277 DAYS

STRANGE CITIES

There are some cities around the world with a lot of very odd stats.

There are a set of tunnels more than **300** kilometres long underneath Paris. They are decorated with human bones.

There are more dogs than children in Seattle.

Istanbul is the only city in the world to be part of **2** continents: Asia and Europe.

200,000

153,000

150,000

107,000

100,000

50,000

0

DOGS   CHILDREN

There are more bicycles than people in Amsterdam.

BICYCLES
881,000

PEOPLE
845,000

There is a street in Prague that is only 50 centimetres wide. That's the same width as these two pages! There is a traffic light at each end to stop people getting stuck as they walk through.

WELCOME
TO Fabulous
LAS VEGAS
NEVADA

There are around 300 weddings every single day in Las Vegas.

VIDEO GAME ARCADES

You can rank all sorts of things with stats. From the number of dogs in one city to how strong the wind is, stats can tell us a lot. We can even find out the cities with the most video game <u>arcades</u> in the world.

STAT ATTACK!

The longest single playthrough of an arcade game was just over 3 ½ days.

There are some cities that have hundreds of video game arcades. For example, Shanghai in China has almost **800** arcades! Here are some cities with lots of video game arcades:

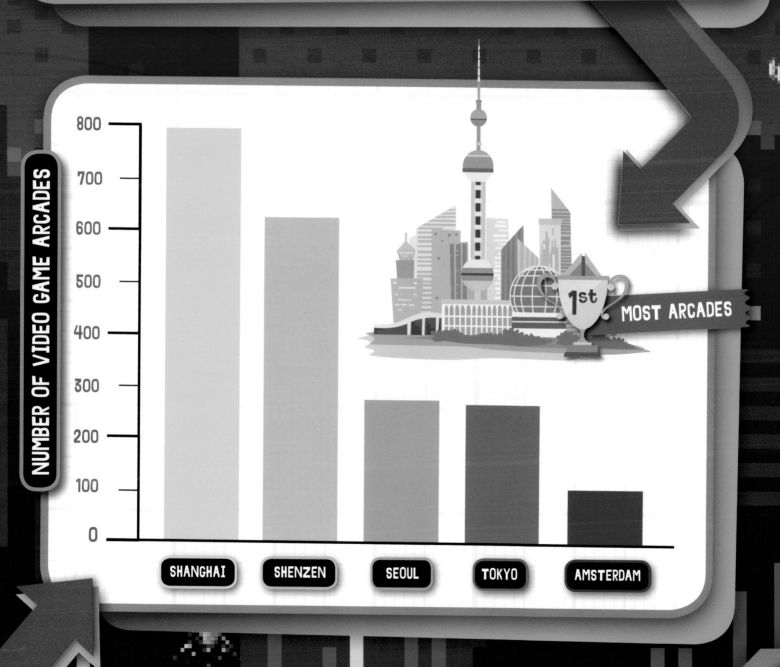

TALLEST BUILDINGS

Some cities have buildings so tall that they seem to reach up through the clouds. These buildings are called skyscrapers. Cities such as New York City, Dubai and Shanghai are famous for their soaring towers. In 2019, the tallest building in the world was the Burj Khalifa in Dubai.

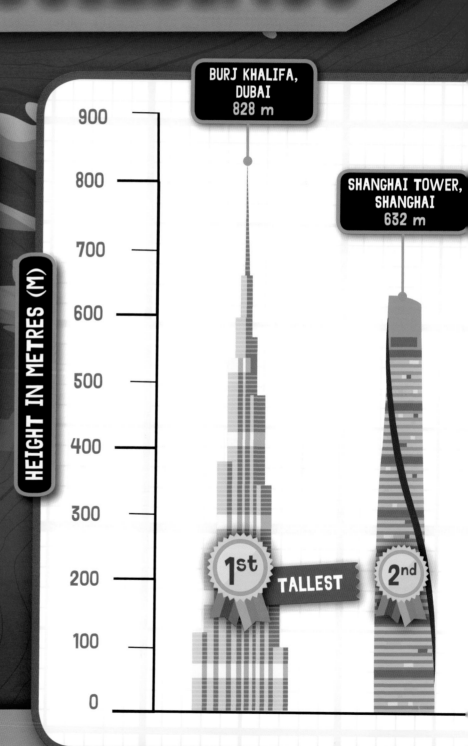

HEIGHT IN METRES (M)

900
800
700
600
500
400
300
200
100
0

BURJ KHALIFA, DUBAI
828 m

SHANGHAI TOWER, SHANGHAI
632 m

1st TALLEST

2nd

New York City is one of the cities with the most skyscrapers. In 2019, it had over **250**.

MAKKAH ROYAL CLOCK
TOWER HOTEL,
MECCA
601 m

PING AN
FINANCE CENTER,
SHENZEN
599 m

LOTTE WORLD TOWER,
SEOUL
555 m

3rd

4th

5th

HOTTEST AND COLDEST

Humans can survive in extreme <u>conditions</u>. Some of the most extreme conditions cities have to cope with are temperatures. The temperature is how hot or cold something is.

The hottest temperature recorded in a city was in Ahvaz, Iran. In 2017, the city reached a temperature of **53.7** degrees Celsius.

IRAN

Ahvaz

The coldest city in the world is in Russia. Yakutsk can reach temperatures as low as **-50** degrees Celsius during the coldest part of winter. That's so cold that people are warned against wearing glasses outside, because they will freeze onto your face!

OLDEST BUILDINGS

Humans have been around for a long time. There are some buildings that were built thousands of years ago that can still be seen today. Many of these buildings are <u>monuments</u> or <u>burial sites</u>.

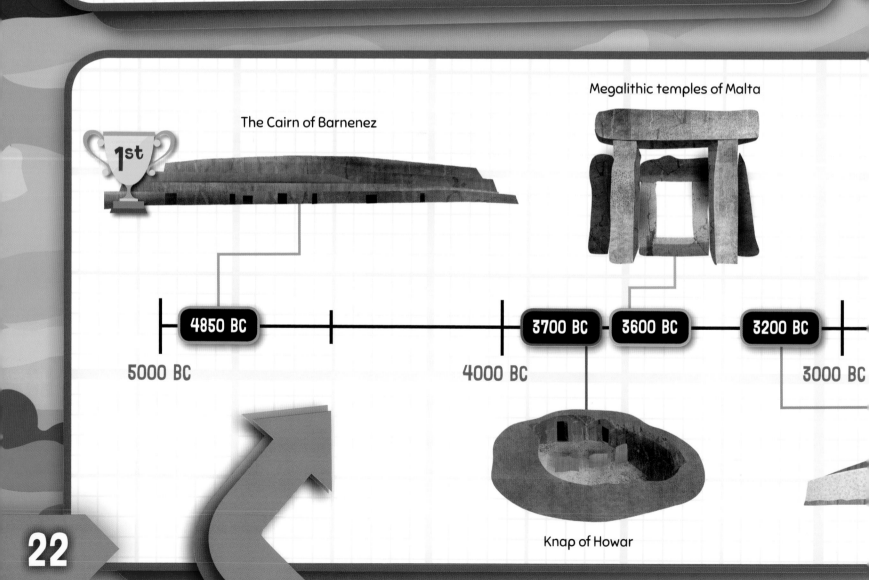

1st

The Cairn of Barnenez

Megalithic temples of Malta

4850 BC

3700 BC **3600 BC** **3200 BC**

5000 BC

4000 BC

3000 BC

Knap of Howar

Some of the oldest buildings in the world date back as far back as 5000 years BC. BC means 'before Christ'. It is used to mark the dates that come before the starting year of most calendars.

Pyramid of Djoser

FACT

We still don't know for certain how Egypt's pyramids were built.

700 BC

2000 BC   0   TODAY

Newgrange of Ireland

GLOSSARY

arcades	places with many video games that can be played, usually by putting coins in
burial sites	places where people are laid to rest after they have died
cathedral	the main church of an area that is headed by a bishop or archbishop
compare	to look at two or more things to see what is similar or different about them
conditions	the state of the environment
government	the group of people who run a country and decide its laws
monuments	things that are built, usually to honour a person or something that happened in history
one-quarter	one of four equal parts of something
represent	to stand for something else
square kilometres	a unit of area equal to a square that is one kilometre long on each side

INDEX